When Mel Fell for Nell

By

D. M. Larson

Copyright (c) 2015   doug@freedrama.net

SCENE 1 - HEART ATTACK

(People are on a subway. A woman, Nell, is standing listening to music. Mel is sitting looking at his watch impatiently. Jay is next to him with a magazine. Lissy sits a ways away reading a book.)

          MEL
How long have we been stuck here? I don't think we've moved at all in an hour. I can't sit here all day. Uh... this is driving me nuts. What's the hold up?

          JAY
No clue. Did you see this article about peace negotiations in North Korea? Kim Jong Un says he'll only talk to Angelina Jolie. Somebody wants a spanking.

          MEL
What? Oh, man.

(Nell looks over at Mel and notices he is in distress)

          JAY
I made that last part up. It doesn't say that.

          MEL
Man... oh...

          JAY
You okay?

          MEL
I... uh... man...

          JAY
You don't look so good.

          MEL
What's wrong with me?

          JAY
Maybe it's something you ate. That egg salad sandwich was not a natural color.

          MEL
Man... Uh! I think this is it... this is that heart attack my doctor
          (MORE)

                      (CONTINUED)

                              MEL (cont'd)
                    promised me... I think this is the
                    big one...

                              JAY
                    Geez... really? Now? Can't you hold
                    it in or something?

                              MEL
                    Oh... oh... man!

(Suddenly Nell goes over to Mel, sits next to him and gives
him a huge kiss. He is startled at first and then calms down
and enjoys it. She stops kissing and Mel looks very happy)

                              NELL
                    There. Better?

                              MEL
                    All better.

                              NELL
                    Good.

(Nell goes back to her spot and listens to her music again.
Mel and Jay look at her in amazement)

                              JAY
                    What was that all about?

                              LISSY
                    You were probably just having a
                    panic attack. She snapped you out
                    of it.

                              MEL
                    I'll say.

                              JAY
                    Panic again... let's see what she
                    does.

(Nell smirks but doesn't look at them)

                              MEL
                    Thank you.

(Nell shrugs)

                              JAY
                    She's hot too. Ask her out.

                    MEL
          What?

                    JAY
          She's hot and she kissed you. Ask
          her out.

                    MEL
          But... I... I'm so confused.

                    JAY
          The kiss was that good huh?

                    MEL
          Better than good. That was the best
          kiss I've had in my whole life.

(Nell smiles to herself and does something flirty with her hair)

                    JAY
          She's flirting. Go for it.

                    MEL
          Uh... uh...

                    JAY
          That's good. Panic. She likes that.

                    MEL
          Stop.

                    JAY
          No, you stop. Stop being so shy.
          Stop missing out on life. Stop
          hiding. Life walked up to you and
          kissed you on the lips. Give life a
          chance. Quit being so dead all the
          time.

                    MEL
          I have been, haven't I? Dead...
          dead for a long time. I can't
          remember the last time I felt
          alive.

                    JAY
          I've known you a long time and I
          can't remember either.

                    MEL
          What happened to me?

(CONTINUED)

CONTINUED:

>   JAY
>   That's the problem. Nothing
>   happened. You never take a chance.
>   You never take a risk. You play it
>   safe and nothing happens to you.
>
>   MEL
>   Until now.
>
>   JAY
>   Until now. And now looks pretty
>   good from where I'm sitting.

(Nell gives Jay a dirty look)

>   JAY (CONT.)
>   She's a firecracker. Go talk to
>   her.
>
>   MEL
>   But what if... I mean if she...
>
>   JAY
>   She kissed you, idiot. She likes
>   you. Go before I kick you in the
>   balls.
>
>   MEL
>   What?
>
>   JAY
>   I will hurt you if you don't go
>   talk to her.
>
>   MEL
>   Fine. Geez.

(Mel goes shyly over to Nell. He isn't sure what to say)

>   NELL
>   Hi. I'm Nell.
>
>   MEL
>   Hi. I'm the guy you kissed... Mel.
>
>   NELL
>   That's a cute name.
>
>   MEL
>   Really?

(CONTINUED)

CONTINUED:

              NELL
Adorable.

              MEL
It's short for Melvin.

              NELL
Even cuter.

              MEL
So... uh... why... uh...

              NELL
Why did I kiss you?

(Mel laughs)

              MEL
Yes.

              NELL
Believe it or not, we ride this subway a lot together. I watch you... because there's something about you that's different from everyone... a sweetness about you. You always give up your seat for women. You even did for me once. If someone forgets a coat or a bag, you get it and chase after them. If a woman is being bugged by some creepy guy and they don't like it, you'll interrupt and make sure the woman safely gets to a taxi, even if the woman doesn't know you're doing it.

              MEL
You saw all that?

              NELL
Yup... I'm a stalker.

(Mel laughs)

              MEL
A good one too. I never noticed.

              NELL
I'm a ninja.

(CONTINUED)

CONTINUED:

          MEL
Ninja stalker. Good combination.

          NELL
Thanks.

          MEL
So that's why you kissed me?

          NELL
Well, in a way. But even though you do all these nice, sweet things, you always look so stressed and unhappy. You look like you're about to have a heart attack at any moment. I see the panic in your eyes sometimes. I see the stress overwhelming you.

          MEL
I didn't think anyone noticed.

          NELL
Not even your friend it appears.

(Jay is checking out Lissy)

          MEL
He has other things on his mind.

          NELL
So I told myself, next time you looked stressed and overwhelmed and on the edge of a heart attack, I was going to give you a great big kiss.

          MEL
That's crazy... and so very nice at the same time.

          NELL
Did you like it?

          MEL
I really liked it. It might be the nicest thing that's ever happened to me.

          NELL
Really? That's the sweetest thing anyone has ever said to me.

(Nell gives Mel another huge kiss)

(CONTINUED)

CONTINUED:

                    MEL
          Wow.

                    NELL
          A wow worthy kiss... I didn't think
          I was that good.

                    MEL
          You are.

                    NELL
          I really enjoy kissing you. I had a
          feeling I would.

                    MEL
          I'm so glad you kissed me.

                    NELL
          I'm so glad you liked it.

                    MEL
          The next car looks empty. Want to
          go over there.

                    NELL
          And do what?

                    MEL
          Uh... well... I just... we can...
          talk.

                    NELL
          Okay.

(Nell takes Mel by the hand and they exit to the next car. Jay goes over to Lissy)

                    JAY
          That was pretty wild huh? Her
          kissing him like that.

                    LISSY
          I thought maybe she was giving a
          free sample or something.

                    JAY
          You think she's "working"?

                    LISSY
          No, I think she is for real. I
          believe her story. I've noticed him
          too. He is a pretty neat guy. He
          deserves to find someone who really
                    (MORE)

                                              (CONTINUED)

                    LISSY (cont'd)
          appreciates him for who he is. I
          think we all noticed him but she
          was the only one willing to say
          anything. Women usually don't make
          the first move. And he's a sweet
          guy so he wouldn't make his move.
          So he was alone... until now. And
          now he looks so happy. That... what
          happened there... was way better
          than this book. Trashy romances
          novels try to give us the perfect
          fantasy but that moment there was
          way better because it was so much
          more real. Give me five minutes of
          seeing that over reading hours of
          this junk.

                    JAY
          So women usually don't make the
          first move huh? They want to be
          pursued, don't they?

                    LISSY
          Out of everything I just said,
          that's all you got out of it.

                    JAY
          Pretty much... so what do you say?

                    LISSY
          Oh, why not.

(Lissy kisses Jay. They end the kiss and look disappointed)

                    LISSY (CONT.)
          I've had better.

                    JAY
          Me too.

(Jay goes back to his magazine and starts reading again. Lissy returns to her novel)

                    END OF SCENE

SCENE 2 - I HATE BUFFETS

				NELL
I hate buffets... Not for the obvious like germs... Get your fingers out of there! Yes I know I'm not your momma.... Just do it... That's gross... Don't you dare lick your fingers.

Gross... Okay maybe it's the germs too...

But here is my main problem. All you can eat is way too much for me... It's too much for everyone.

Why do we need so many options? I hate all these choices. And I always feel like I make the wrong one.

I eat something and it sits like a lump in my stomach... I try another... Two lumps. Another... It's all terrible... Buffets don't give you more... Just a lot of bad choices... I just want to find one place... A great place with something really good. One really good thing I can count on to always be good for me. So yummy I will just eat it over and over again... That one wonderful thing that settles inside me...

(Burps or almost throws up...)
Not this... This torture... Eating and eating bits of everything... Tearing me up inside... It's gonna rip me apart.

				END OF SCENE

SCENE 3 - LOVE AT THE INTERNATIONAL FUSION CAFE

(Waiters can be either gender and even be two actors doing multiple costumes. Mario leads Mel and Nell to a table in the restaurant)

          MARIO
Welcome to the International Fusion Cafe where we bring a tour of the world to your taste buds. Have you ever dined with us before?

          MEL
I have. She hasn't.

          MARIO
Let me enlighten the señorita to our ways.

          NELL
This isn't some weird cult you are making me join is it?

          MEL
You wanted unique. I am giving you the unique-est.

          MARIO
This is like a buffet but instead of you getting your foods, we bring the foods to you.

(He gets a plate)

          MARIO (CONT.)
We will bring some food like so.... I call it "That's a spicy meatball!" And if you like it, we serve it to you.

          NELL
Interesting... Lay some meatballs on me Mario.

          MARIO
You sir?

          MEL
Cows and I don't get along. I will pass.

(CONTINUED)

CONTINUED:

>   MARIO
> It may not be cows in the meatball.
> I'm not sure.

>   NELL
> You don't know? I will pass too.
> Don't bother sending Luigi with any
> mushrooms. I hate those too.

(Mario leaves in a huff)

>   MEL
> Weird eh?

(Batman appears)

>   NELL
> No, not at all.

>   BATMAN
> Would the lady enjoy some fried bat
> wings?

>   NELL
> Ewwww... No.

>   MEL
> They're chicken wings...

(Batman gives him some)

>   MEL (cont'd)
> At least I think so.

>   BATMAN
> They taste like chicken.

>   NELL
> Fine. I will nibble on a bat wing
> or two. I can pretend I am Ozzy
> Osborne.

>   MEL
> They should call it the Ozzy
> special.

>   NELL
> I thought you didn't like Ozzy...

>   MEL
> Not really...

(CONTINUED)

CONTINUED:

>NELL
>Why won't you give my music a chance?

>MEL
>Ozzy isn't music. It's noise.

>NELL
>Hey!

>MEL
>Just kidding... And besides, aren't you too young to like Ozzy?

>NELL
>I like the classics. The Doors, Pink Floyd.

(Mel rolls his eyes)

>NELL (cont'd)
>Don't roll your eyes at Pink Floyd. I am trying your bizarre restaurant.

(A mime passes through being pulled on an invisible rope. Nell stands up)

>NELL (CONT.)
>You better try my music... Or I am leaving.

>MEL
>Sit down. I will listen to your music. I promise.

(Nell looks very pleased with herself and sits)

>NELL
>Good.

>MEL
>Why do you do that?

>NELL
>What?

>MEL
>Pretend to throw a fit to get your way. I thought you were serious.

(CONTINUED)

CONTINUED:

                    NELL
          I was serious.

                    MEL
          Was that really worth making a
          scene about?

                    NELL
          Maybe. It was fun.

                    MEL
          For you maybe.

                    NELL
          You need to lighten up. That's my
          mission in life. To lighten your
          load.

                    MEL
          You do actually.

                    NELL
          Really?

                    MEL
          Yeah.

                    NELL
          Tell me about it.

                    MEL
          Huh?

                    NELL
          Share with me. Open up. Tell me
          what you like about me.

                    MEL
          Here? Now?

                    NELL
          Now... Or the mime gets it.

(Points an imaginary weapon at mime as he approaches)

                    MEL
          Crossbow! Nice.

(Mime lowers her imaginary weapon and holds out a covered plate)

(CONTINUED)

CONTINUED:

NELL
French food maybe?

(Mime nods and opens dish. It's empty)

MEL
Oh good. Its their low calorie menu.

(Mime does a silent laugh and gets a real plate)

NELL
French bread?

(Mime nods)

NELL (cont'd)
How clever.

(They both take some. Mel is looking at Nell in a dreamy state)

NELL (cont'd)
Okay, what are you thinking?

(Mel gets embarrassed)

MEL
Oh no, I can't.

NELL
If you want this relationship to work I need some open and honest communication.

MEL
What I was thinking would be a little too open and honest.

NELL
Try me.

MEL
It's embarrassing.

NELL
Tell me now!

(She points her imaginary crossbow at him)

MEL
Well... Umm... Mimes are from France...

(CONTINUED)

CONTINUED:

                    NELL
          Uh huh.

                    MEL
          And I was thinking you'd look nice
          in something French.

                    NELL
          This is good... Like what?

                    MEL
          This is really embarrassing.

                    NELL
          Come on... Please.

                    MEL
          You'll think I'm a pervert.

                    NELL
          I know you're a pervert - now tell
          me!

                    MEL
          I was thinking you'd look good
          dressed as a French maid.

                    NELL
          What?! Oh my!

                    MEL
          I told you it was bad.

                    NELL
          I'd do it.

                    MEL
          Huh?

                    NELL
          I would dress as a French maid for
          you.

     (Mel gets a little too excited)

                    MEL
          You would! I mean... You would?

                    NELL
          Maybe... If you say something nice
          to me.

(CONTINUED)

CONTINUED:

>   MEL
>   I think a lot of nice things...

>   NELL
>   Then say them to me.

>   MEL
>   I get shy.

>   NELL
>   I know and that's so cute. Damn
>   you.

>   MEL
>   Ok... Something nice. Here goes...

(Clown enters)

>   CLOWN
>   'Ello governor

(Mel jumps)

>   MEL
>   Ah! When did you guys get a clown?

>   CLOWN
>   I'm new.

>   NELL
>   You're not very... Silly.

>   CLOWN
>   I am one of them sad clowns.

>   NELL
>   Sad indeed.

>   CLOWN
>   Quite.

>   MEL
>   Why are you British?

>   CLOWN
>   Cause clowns originated in England.
>   The first clown was portrayed by
>   Joseph Gronaldi in the early
>   1800s...

>   NELL
>   You clowns tell the funniest
>   stories.

(CONTINUED)

CONTINUED:

            MEL
You got any good to go with your
delightful history lesson?

            CLOWN
Fish and chips.

            NELL
Do the British eat anything else?

            CLOWN
Not really ma'am, no.

(Clown leaves)

            NELL
A very sad clown indeed... And
you're not off the hook. Share some
feelings.... Now!

            MEL
Ok... Uh... Well...

            NELL
Oh never mind. Don't hurt yourself.

            MEL
I really want to... I really do...
You mean a lot to me and I want you
to know that. I mean I have never
been so happy in my life. You have
made everything so much better. I
look forward to every day I get to
be with you. I want to tell you all
that. I just can't seem to do it.

            NELL
You just did.

(She sits on his lap and gives him a hug and a kiss)

            MEL
I am very happy now too.

            NELL
I can tell.

            MEL
How embarrassing.

            NELL
Is that guy in the kilt serving
haggis?

(CONTINUED)

MEL
Haggis! Awesome. The national food of Scotland. You're Scottish aren't you? How come you never wear a kilt?

NELL
You'd like that huh? But that means I would be a guy.

MEL
I wouldn't like that.

NELL
I have always wanted to go to Scotland. Wouldn't that be a great place for our honeymoon?

MEL
What?

NELL
Scotland... Travel... Fun.

MEL
No, the other part.

NELL
What? Me being a guy?

MEL
You said our honeymoon.

NELL
I did?

MEL
Yes.

NELL
No, I didn't.

MEL
Little early to be talking about honeymoons... We haven't even discussed weddings yet... Or engagements.

NELL
Can we talk about something else?

(CONTINUED)

CONTINUED: 19.

              MEL
Uh... Ok... I mean... I don't mind talking about it but if you don't want to.

              NELL
I don't.

(Silence. Mime comes by with food... He tries to get their attention with invisible flowers but they are quiet and ignore him. He tries harder but Nell takes his invisible flowers he is playing with, wads then in to a ball and throws them. He leaves in frustration)

              NELL (cont'd)
I am curious though...

              MEL
Yes?

              NELL
Would you marry me?

              MEL
Are you proposing?

              NELL
What? No!

              MEL
But you said "would you marry me?"

              NELL
Stop putting words in my mouth.

              MEL
I wouldn't say no.

              NELL
Really?

              MEL
Really.

              NELL
Oh.

              MEL
Yeah.

              NELL
Wanna go back to my place?

(CONTINUED)

CONTINUED: 20.

                    MEL
Yes.

                    NELL
Let's go.

(Mime comes up and stops them and holds out an invisible bill. Mel takes out an invisible check book. Writes the check, rips it out and gives invisible check to mime. They wave at him and they leave. He is sad and does a silent fit. Nell returns and shoots him with her invisible cross bow. Mime falls down dead)

                    MEL
If a tree falls in the forest and falls on a mime, does anyone care?

                    NELL
That's deep.

                    MEL
Quite.

                    NELL
So would you wear a kilt for me?

                    MEL
If you dress as a French maid.

(They laugh and exit. Batman goes up to the mime)

                    BATMAN
A mime is a terrible thing to waste.

                END OF SCENE

SCENE 4 - BREAKING HEART

NELL
You want to break up... sure... no problem... yeah, I wanted to break up too. I've been thinking about it from the day we met. This is a person I will need to break up with. But hey... you beat me to it. No hard feelings.

(Shrugs and turns away)
Be friends?

(Turns with a huge smile)
Sure! I'd love to be friends. That's the natural evolution of most relationships. Have a fling and then boom... friends. I'm sure some of the best friendships started that way.

(Overly enthusiastic)
I look forward to hanging out with you, buddy. Let's meet up and go to Hooters or football or something some time and hang out.
(yells) That would be GREAT!

(Quiet/angry/eyes closed)
What? Upset? No, I'm not upset. Why would I be... upset...

(Starts to cry)
No, I'm not crying. I said, I'm not crying!

(Bursts in to tears)
I don't want your pity. I don't want a shoulder to cry on. I want... to be left...

(Yells)
...ALONE! Don't you get it. I want to be alone!

(Pauses... sadly reflects)
I've always wanted to be alone. I never wanted to get close to anyone. I never wanted us to get close. And I guess I was closer to you than you were to me.

(Turns angry)

(CONTINUED)

CONTINUED: 22.

>   Don't lie to me. I know you don't
>   mean it. I don't want to hear any
>   more lies! I don't want you to make
>   something up so you can get out of
>   this. I want it all laid out on the
>   table.
>
> (Yells)
>   I want to know the truth!
>
> (Long pause... cries... then manages to say)
>   I want to know why you are breaking
>   my heart.

                    END OF SCENE

SCENE 5 - ONE WAY OR ANOTHER

(Mel is outside Nell's house. Her bedroom is on the second floor. He throws some pebbles up to get her attention [or he can have a boom box playing a song and holding it over his head]. Nell comes out annoyed)

NELL
What are you doing out here?

MEL
I wanted to say hi.

NELL
Hi... bye.

MEL
You look good.

NELL
Yeah, so?

MEL
Very good.

NELL
Stop it.

MEL
What?

NELL
We broke up, remember?

MEL
Yeah.

NELL
YOU broke up with me.

MEL
Yeah... you still look good.

NELL
What's wrong?

MEL
I miss you.

NELL
Well... I could be mean about it... and take pleasure you in saying that... and torment you... but... I miss you too...

(CONTINUED)

CONTINUED: 24.

                    MEL
          You do?

                    NELL
          Yeah...

                    MEL
          Can I come in?

                    NELL
          No.

                    MEL
          Please.

                    NELL
          Go away.

                    MEL
          But you miss me.

                    NELL
          Not that much.

                    MEL
          I guess I shouldn't have gotten you
          anything then.

                    NELL
          You got me something?

                    MEL
          Never mind... I'll go.

                    NELL
          But...you got me something.

                    MEL
          It's not much.

                    NELL
          What is it?

                    MEL
          You want to see?

                    NELL
          Yes.

                    MEL
          Can I come in?

(CONTINUED)

CONTINUED: 25.

			NELL
	No.

			MEL
	Please.

			NELL
	Hold it up and I'll grab it.

			MEL
	Really?

			NELL
	Yeah.

(Mel tries to reach but they can't so he starts to climb up. She manages to grab it and he falls)

			MEL
	Ah!

			NELL
	You okay?

			MEL
	...maybe.

			NELL
	You're hurt?

			MEL
	...no... not much.

			NELL
	You look hurt.

			MEL
	No... I'm fine.

			NELL
	Why are you still in the bushes then?

			MEL
	It's comfortable. Think I'll just stay here a bit... enjoy the gift.

			NELL
	I'm coming down.

			MEL
	No, no... I don't want to bug you... see you later... I'm sure
			(MORE)

					(CONTINUED)

CONTINUED: 26.

>   MEL (cont'd)
>   I'll be gone by morning. One way or
>   another.

(Nell appears out front door and goes to bushes. She struggles to get him out)

>   NELL
>   You are hurt.

>   MEL
>   That's not blood... that's
>   uh...ketchup... had some fries on
>   the way over.

>   NELL
>   I didn't think you fell that far.

>   MEL
>   I'm accident prone.

>   NELL
>   I know. You need a keeper.

>   MEL
>   Want to be my keeper again?

(He snuggles up to her)

>   NELL
>   No.

(She drops him)

>   MEL
>   Ow.

>   NELL
>   Sorry.

(She helps him up)

>   MEL
>   You don't have to be nice to me
>   anymore.

>   NELL
>   I'll always be nice to you.

>   MEL
>   Really? But I broke up with you.

(CONTINUED)

CONTINUED:

> NELL
> That's right. I guess I should be a little meaner. Good night.

> MEL
> You're leaving?

> NELL
> You're not hurt that badly.

> MEL
> Right.

> NELL
> See ya.

(She shuts the front door. Mel tries standing and is in pain. His leg is probably broken. He struggles to walk but fails gloriously and falls. He crawls off dramatically. Suddenly there is a gasp of happiness and Nell rushes out on to the balcony)

> NELL (CONT.)
> Mel? Mel, you there?

> MEL (OFF)
> Maybe.

> NELL
> Where did you find these?

(Mel tries to walk in like he isn't hurt)

> MEL
> Oh those? No big deal. Just found them.

> NELL
> These are my favorite chocolates... they only sell these in Europe.

> MEL
> Oh, really?

> NELL
> Shut up. You knew.

> MEL
> You always carry on about them. Always wanted to get them for you.

(CONTINUED)

CONTINUED:

              NELL
Why now?

              MEL
Why now...

(Mel turns sadly and starts to walk away and falls dramatically)

              NELL
Oh no.

(Nell runs down. She runs out front door to him)

              MEL
I'm sorry. I didn't want to do this to you.

              NELL
Then why are you?

              MEL
Because I miss you. I thought I was doing the right thing, but I miss you.

              NELL
I miss you too... but it hurt.

              MEL
I know.

              NELL
You said so many things that hurt.

              MEL
I thought you'd be better off without me.

              NELL
And you thought you'd be better off without me.

              MEL
But I'm not.

(Nell holds him)

              NELL
What am I going to do with you?

(CONTINUED)

CONTINUED:

> MEL
> What am I going to do without you?

> NELL
> How about I just sit here and hold you for awhile?

> MEL
> I'd like that.

(Nell holds Mel closer. They look at the stars)

END OF SCENE

SCENE 6 - DUMMY

                    MEL
          This is not me.

          (Points to self.)

          This is me over here.

(Points to dummy)
          He can't say the right thing so I
          have to speak for him. You know
          those people who always say the
          wrong thing at the worst moment in
          the worst possible way? Well that's
          me... Well, him... Us... We. Not
          the royal we either.

(Turns to dummy like he said something)
          Babbling? Yes... Thanks dummy... I
          will get to the point. I didn't
          mean to stop talking to you... I
          didn't mean to turn in to him over
          there... But I just wanted to stop
          ... Stop before I did any more
          damage. It feels like my words
          cause so much destruction. It's
          like a flower in the wind. You love
          the gentle breeze of my words when
          I say sweet things to you... You
          open yourself up and bloom for me
          in my kindest moments. But the
          harsh words break you and tear you
          apart like a storm. My words storm
          and rage over you like some black
          cloud raining over us ripping the
          gentle petals from you. Like a
          flower caught in a tornado.

          I want to whisper sweet things
          again. I want to nourish you and
          help you grow your beautiful
          blossom again, but I get so scared
          ... I become so afraid of what I
          will do. You deserve kindness...
          Upon deserve beauty. You deserve
          loving words. I want that too. But
          I feel silenced. I feel crippled
          inside. I feel broken.

          There are so many things I want to
          say to you though. So many
          wonderful things I feel for you...
          See in you... Get from you.

                                              (CONTINUED)

CONTINUED:

> I feel better because of you. Like you healed me in some way. I felt sick emotionally before I had you in my life. I felt spiritually dead. You brought me back to life, resurrected the spirit inside me, healed me. You're my angel. That's what you are to me. An angel. So delicate. Such a pure spirit. No hardness hiding the goodness and purity. You leave yourself open to me, giving your full self to me, hiding nothing. You give everything to me... And keep nothing for yourself. You give me your wings so I can fly. You'd remove your heart just to keep mine beating.
>
> You are the greatest gift that has ever been given to me. You complete me. You make me whole.
>
> I wish I could speak those words to you.
>
> (Looks at dummy)
> I wish this dummy could say what I feel.

END OF SCENE

SCENE 7 - LATE

(Carl is a service station worker who is sitting with a clipboard waiting for customers. Mel rushes in)

>					MEL
> I'm so sorry I'm late.

>					CARL
> What time was your appointment?

(Mel hands over his keys to Carl. During the following, Carl tags the keys and then can hand off the keys to another worker or he can rush the keys off stage or put it on a line and push the keys on the line off stage)

>					MEL
> It was 30 minutes ago. I'm never late. I'm so sorry about this. I'd understand if you can fit me in now.

>					CARL
> No worries we got you covered.

>					MEL
> Now I'm late for work. I hate being late for work. It's not that I will get fired; it's more that they look at you a different way. They give you this look... you're not as good as us, or we have one up on you, or we have something we can use against you. I always try to play it straight. Always on time. Never late. I'm so late today. I sometimes wish I could be a slacker. What's that like?

(Carl has been sitting relaxed, listening, eating a doughnut)

>					CARL
> Hard to say. Need a ride to work?

>					MEL
> Will it be awhile? Something wrong with my car? Figures. Everything is going wrong. Everything's so right then it goes so wrong. Well, that's not true. I hate to sound that way. Is it really that bad?

(CONTINUED)

CONTINUED:

>   CARL
>   You bring in your car pretty
>   regular. I don't see a need to
>   worry.
>
>   MEL
>   That's me. Mr. Do-right. Most my
>   life it was Mr. Do-right But it was
>   getting to me. Really getting to
>   me. I thought I was going to have a
>   heart attack. How could following
>   the rules so perfectly make me so
>   perfectly stressed? Shouldn't right
>   be... right? But it didn't feel
>   right. I was so unhappy. I just
>   wanted to be happy for once. Just
>   have one little bit of happiness
>   for the first time in my life.

(Mel pauses and looks at Carl. Carl is listening, quite curious about what Mel is talking about)

>   MEL (CONT.)
>   You want to know why I'm late?
>
>   CARL
>   Of course.
>
>   MEL
>   I am late because my girlfriend is
>   late.
>
>   CARL
>   Late? Ohhhh... late. I see.
>
>   MEL
>   Yeah, that kind of late. The kind
>   of late that changes your life and
>   you can't go back.
>
>   CARL
>   Well... you can but...
>
>   MEL
>   No. No way. We're not considering
>   that. Never.
>
>   CARL
>   So what are you going to do?
>
>   MEL
>   She really wants the baby. She
>   actually thought she couldn't have
>   (MORE)

(CONTINUED)

MEL (cont'd)
one and she's so happy she can. Well, she's freaking out, but happy.

CARL
Makes sense.

MEL
I want to be happy to, but all these worries keep making it so hard. That's not fair to her...

CARL
Or yourself.

MEL
I tend to forget about me.

CARL
Not a good idea. If we don't take care of ourselves then we can't help anyone else.

MEL
Especially not a baby. Am I ready to be a father?

CARL
It changes your life.

MEL
I've never changed anything. I always do the same thing. I get up at 5am. Eat the same breakfast. Get to work the same time... usually. Get my car serviced once a month.

CARL
I'm thankful for that one.

MEL
But this... this changes everything.

CARL
Get ready for an adventure.

MEL
Adventure... That's a scary word.

(CONTINUED)

CONTINUED:

              CARL
Really? I love that word. I want every day to be an adventure.

              MEL
Every day! I'd go crazy. Every day I want the same thing. I want to know what's coming.

              CARL
Do you want it? Need it? Or just do it because seems right? Before today, what was the last thing you did that wasn't planned or scheduled?

              MEL
Kissed a beautiful woman I didn't even know... or rather got kissed by her.

              CARL
How did it feel?

              MEL
Scary... crazy... But it was memorable... the best kiss ever. I'll never forget it. And I never stopped kissing her. I guess that's why she's late.

              CARL
Do that think it changed you?

              MEL
Totally.

              CARL
For the better?

              MEL
Yes. Things have never been the same. And they've gotten better. I actually feel happy sometimes. I never really felt happy before. But now I do. I didn't know I was missing some happy until I got some.

              CARL
Kids do that too. They make every day a new experience. And it's amazing to see the world through
            (MORE)

(CONTINUED)

CONTINUED: 36.

                CARL (cont'd)
their eyes. I think we learn more from them than they do from us. You're in for an adventure my friend.

(Carl gets the keys returned the same way he sent them)

                MEL
There's that word again. Adventure. Maybe it's time I had some in my life. Playing it safe got me nothing but a job I hate and an ulcer. Thanks for listening. I kind of unloaded on you.

                CARL
No problemo. Happy to help. Here's the bill. Therapy would have been cheaper I think.

(Carl hands over the bill)

                MEL
Funny.

                CARL
I thought so. Hopefully you're not too late for work.

                MEL
I'm calling in sick.

                CARL
You're kidding?

                MEL
I have a beautiful woman to kiss and a baby to celebrate.

(Mel exits)

                CARL
Don't forget to bring us all some cigars! I wonder if anyone actually does that anymore? My cousin handed out lollipops when his kid was born. I wanted to punch him.

              END OF SCENE

SCENE 8 - WAITING ON THE BRIDE

              MEL

Where is she? The ceremony starts soon and she's not even here. I hope something didn't happen to her. The one time we don't go somewhere together and something happens.

She's not calling or texting. That's not good. It might be bad. Really bad.

I wonder if someone can find out if there are any accidents near here. I wish I hadn't picked that hotel for her across town. I should have looked harder for something closer to the church.

This is terrible. I couldn't live with myself if something happened to her. I should have bought her a safer car. I didn't check the safety rating when we bought it. It's so small. What if some big truck...

Stop! ...don't think about it.

Think about something else... The honeymoon... The honeymoon will be so nice... A week away with no body bugging us.

What if she is late and we don't make the flight? What if she isn't coming at all? I know she loves me but I know this has all been so stressful ... Maybe it got to be too much for her... Does she really want to add all my baggage to her life? I wouldn't wish my problems on anyone. She's a pretty amazing person to put up with it all. But maybe it got to be too much when thought about being stuck with my problems...

Stuck... Forever... Scary words... No wonder she ran away... I never wanted her to feel stuck... I
         (MORE)

(CONTINUED)

MEL (cont'd)
wanted to feel free... But she is like a beautiful song bird you have in your home but you decide it might be better for her if you let her go. You open the cage but she doesn't fly away... She stays with you singing her wonderful song, making every day more beautiful with her presence...

Is she here? Thank you God she is here... I am getting married... I really am... Why am I so nervous? I can't wait to see her... She must be so beautiful today... I am a lucky guy... How did I get so lucky? I can't wait to spend the rest of my life with her. I'm so happy she wants that too.

END OF SCENE

SCENE 9 - STEALING MOMENTS

(The scene begins in an empty living room with a sofa in the middle. It's night. Mel and Nell back toward each other slowly away from something scary in front of them on each side of the stage. They stop when they meet in the middle, back to back, looking scared at something off each side of the stage)

                    NELL
I think the baby is finally asleep.

                    MEL
The terrible two is too.

                    NELL
And we're actually awake.

                    MEL
What do we do?

(Nell turns and faces Mel. Taps him on the shoulder and he turns)

                    NELL
I think this is our first moment alone since the baby was born.

                    MEL
Who are you again?

                    NELL
Nice to meet you. I'm Nell.

                    MEL
And I'm Mel. Come here often?

                    NELL
Not often enough.

                    MEL
Did it hurt?

                    NELL
Did what hurt?

                    MEL
When you fell down from heaven?

                    NELL
Blah... worst pick up line ever.

(CONTINUED)

CONTINUED:

>MEL
>Well, you look like an angel to me.

>NELL
>Oh stop.

(Nell sits on the sofa. Mel joins her)

>MEL
>Would it be too forward to ask for a kiss?

>NELL
>But we just met.

>MEL
>No, we have met before... once upon a dream.

>NELL
>A grown man quoting Sleeping Beauty is not romantic.

>MEL
>But I love kissing you when you're asleep.

>NELL
>That's about the only chance we get.

>MEL
>How about now?

>NELL
>Dare we?

>MEL
>I'll check on the kids.

(Mel sneaks up to each side of the stage and checks the sleeping kids)

>MEL (CONT.)
>They're asleep.

>NELL
>It's been so long. Kiss me you fool.

(They go in slowly for a kiss and the baby cries)

(CONTINUED)

CONTINUED:

                MEL
How does she know?

                NELL
She doesn't want any more babies in the house.

                MEL
It's working.

                NELL
She's quiet again.

                MEL
Dare we try?

                NELL
I'm scared.

(They lean in for a kiss - baby cries - they move apart - baby stops crying - they look at each other puzzled - Mel holds out his hand to Nell - baby cries - he quickly pulls away - baby stops crying - she sticks out her hand quickly and back again - baby does a quick cry along with her)

                MEL
This is crazy.

                NELL
Maybe we should just go to bed.

(He looks hopeful)

                NELL (CONT.)
And sleep.

(He looks sad)

                NELL (CONT.) (cont'd)
She won't let us do that either.

(Nell drags Mel after her. They stop at one side of the stage)

                MEL
Being a parent is so hard.

                NELL
But look at her sleeping - she's so beautiful.

(Mel gives Nell a kiss on the cheek)

                (CONTINUED)

CONTINUED: 42.

                    MEL
          Ha - I snuck that one in.

                    NELL
          She didn't cry.

                    MEL
          Let's see what else we can sneak
          in.

(They hold hands and rush to the bedroom - silence a few   moments - then a cry)

                    END OF SCENE

SCENE 10 - FOREVER ON HOLD

                    NELL
          Doesn't it always seem like we're
          on hold? We constantly are calling
          about this or that. We are slaves
          to the phone, waiting anxiously for
          a human voice.

          Companies try to make your
          experience pleasant by playing
          music. One company I called even
          had its own radio station dedicated
          to entertaining people on hold. My
          question is, "Why not make that
          person answer phones too?" There
          are probably more people working on
          message systems that put people on
          hold than there are answering
          phones.

          I especially hate the ones that
          make you feel like you're getting
          somewhere when you actually aren't.
          They come up with all these phrases
          that keep you interested:

(Does a mock answering machine voice)
          "Only a few moments more... ring,
          ring... You have just advanced in
          our waiting order. Beep. Hello (big
          pause) you are the next caller. Do
          not hang up. We will be with you in
          a moment...after 10 more minutes...
          We will be with you in a moment.
          You are the next caller."

          The most aggravating award goes to
          the electronic maze of number
          choices:

(Mock answering machine voice)
          "Press one if you need customer
          assistance. Press two if you need
          customer information. Press three
          if you need customer guidance.
          Press four for more options."

          You wade endlessly through this
          maze of choices only to discover
          you still have to wait an hour to
          talk to someone.

                    (MORE)

                                              (CONTINUED)

CONTINUED:

                    NELL (cont'd)

Then there's the notorious dead line. You wonder, "Did they hang up? Is someone there waiting for you to speak? Did they transfer your call to Albania?" You wait, unsure what to do.

When you finally get to talk to someone, you discover it's not even the right department. They have no clue what you are talking about and transfer you to someone who is equally clueless. Also while you were waiting they ask you to type in your account number, zip code, date of birth, then when you actually talk to a human, they ask you all over again. THEN WHY DID I JUST TYPE THAT IN! When talking to a human, we know why it takes so long. They ask you a million useless questions, they find out YOUR question and transfer you to someone who goes through the same things only to discover they have no clue how to help you either!

Finally someone helps you and you end up receiving a six month subscription to Dog's Life Magazine. At least you got something for all your trouble, but wasn't that supposed to be your credit card company?

                      END OF SCENE

SCENE 11 - HIPSTER HOBOS

(Mel and Nell enter the seating area of a restaurant with a tray filled with drinks, a number and dinner rolls. They are talking so they don't notice immediately that all the tables are taken by a person a each table with a laptop or tablet or some electronic device)

          NELL
You think the kids are okay?

          MEL
We have a good sitter.

          NELL
Why do they have to act that way when I leave? They act like they are dying. Why do they have to be so over-dramatic? It's worse than watching Titanic.

          MEL
No... nothing is worse than watching Titanic.

(They realize they are wandering a bit too much)

          NELL
All the tables are taken.

          MEL
Oh no. It's the hipster hobos.

          NELL
The what?

          MEL
Hipster hobos... aka laptop hobos... they find hip places with free wifi and buy the cheapest thing possible and camp out for the entire day.

          NELL
Don't they have anything better to do?

          MEL
No... this is their life. Taking up space and trying to look cool while doing it.

(CONTINUED)

CONTINUED:

>
> NELL
> Well... it's not cool. I am a tired mom who needs a night to relax... I just need to sit.
>
> MEL
> I think that one's asleep. Maybe if we sit with her really quiet.
>
> NELL
> I want our own table. I think that one ran out of battery... oh, wait, he has an extension cord.
>
> MEL
> You think with all the free refills they'd have to get up to go pee more.
>
> NELL
> Maybe if I find the wifi hub, I can unplug it.
>
> MEL
> And get us kicked out.
>
> NELL
> Why don't they kick them out?
>
> MEL
> It's a vicious cycle. This restaurant wants to appear hip. So they want the hipsters in here to draw in the rest of the hip crowd. But hipsters have to fit in their skinny jeans so they don't buy much food.
>
> NELL
> I have an idea.

(Nell speaks loudly)

>
> NELL (CONT.)
> Did you hear about the sale at the Apple store?! It's a good one!

(Hipsters start to take interest)

>
> NELL (CONT.) (cont'd)
> They have a sale on the new iPid!

(CONTINUED)

CONTINUED:

                    HIPSTER 1
          The iPid?

                    HIPSTER 2
          What's an iPid?

(Hipsters start to stir and get excited)

                    NELL (CONT.)
          I don't know! But it's new!

                    HIPSTER 3
          I need one!

                    HIPSTER 4
          Me too!

(Hipsters start to pack up in a hurry and leave)

                    NELL (CONT.)
          And I hear they will give 100 iPids
          away to the first 100 people in
          line.

(Hipsters are leaving)

                    NELL (CONT.) (cont'd)
          They don't open until morning so
          you'll have to wait in line all
          night.

                    HIPSTER 1
          I always stay in line the night
          before the launch of a new Apple
          product.

                    HIPSTER 2
          Who doesn't?

(Hipster 3 calls out to a waitress off stage)

                    HIPSTER 3
          I brought my extension cord. Is it
          okay if I leave it plugged in here?

                    HIPSTER 4
          I have a power strip.

(All the Hipsters are gone. Nell smiles big)

                    NELL
          Which table would you like?

                                        (CONTINUED)

CONTINUED: 48.

(They sit down happily and Nell unplugs the long extension cord that was left behind by the hipsters. Blackout. Hipsters moan and groan in the darkness)

END OF SCENE

SCENE 12 - THE MEANING OF LIFE

>   MEL
> So much of my life I was searching... Missing something. I was a wanderer... Lost in the desert without you... Seeking nourishment but getting a mouthful of sand. Catching glimpses of you... Thinking you were a lovely mirage in the heat of madness. Something I would never be able to hold on to. A fantasy... Some trick of the light.
>
> But you are real. More real than my life before... My past a nightmare... My future a never ending dream because of you.
>
> When I found you... truly found you... I knew you would make my life complete. You complete me... Make me whole. You are the missing piece of the puzzle that made the full portrait of me. Finally there is meaning to it all. The meaning of life is no longer a mystery. The meaning is life is you.
>
> You are the reward ... The gift after the sacrifice. Freedom from the slavery of my past.
>
> In you I find the freedom to be who I really am. Safe to be myself. Safe to love and grow in spirit, sheltered in your loving embrace.
>
>   END

SCENE 13 - FALLING AWAY FROM YOU

(Mel is alone in a busy street. There are sounds of crowds of people. There are cars honking. Mel wants to cross the street but cars are rushing by. He acts like invisible people are pushing him. He gets in a panic. Nell appears and the noises stop. Mel sees her and runs to her. She wants to hug him but can't because of some invisible barrier)

     MEL
Every time I fly, I wonder why I'm flying. Especially when I'm flying alone. What's the point of going if I leave you behind? What if you're not there when I get back?

     NELL
Do you really worry about that?

     MEL
I worry about everything.

     NELL
Why now? I thought you were better.

     MEL
I am. I was. Most of the time...

     NELL
Are you okay?

     MEL
Not really.

     NELL
Is it that hard for you?

     MEL
Everything is hard for me... well, it was... you make it easier... I thought I would be okay on my own... but you're my anchor. You keep me steady.

     NELL
I want to. Is it that hard without me?

     MEL
I feel like I'm in a fog. Slightly out of sync. I'm here, on this crowded street but I don't really see anyone. They don't see me either.

(CONTINUED)

CONTINUED: 51.

                    NELL
          I see you.

                    MEL
          You always do.

                    NELL
          I see so much more than you see
          yourself.

                    MEL
          I want to be that person you see. I
          really do...

                    NELL
          Then be that person.

                    MEL
          I'm scared.

                    NELL
          Of what?

                    MEL
          I don't know. Everything. The world
          scares me.

(Sirens)

                    MEL (CONT.)
          What is that?

                    NELL
          What do you hear?

                    MEL
          Sirens? Strange sirens.

(Sirens mix with cries)

                    MEL (CONT.)
          Strange sounds. Echoing through the
          city. The empty city. It like I
          don't see anyone but I know they
          are there. I feel crowded but
          alone.

                    NELL
          I'm here, Mel. You don't have to be
          afraid. The sirens stop.

                                                              (CONTINUED)

CONTINUED:

                    MEL
          How can you be here? We said
          good-bye. I hate saying good-bye.
          Those tears... those tears in your
          beautiful eyes.

                    NELL
          Those tears are because I love you.
          I don't cry for anyone else. Tears
          aren't always bad... I cried when
          we first made love.

                    MEL
          You did. I was worried I'd hurt
          you.

                    NELL
          No, never. It was so nice... I
          cried.

                    MEL
          Tears...

                    NELL
          Tears of love.

                    MEL
          Have there been too many tears?
          Have you cried too much?

                    NELL
          I love the way you touch me inside.
          I was frozen once. The ice queen.
          No one could penetrate. But you
          did... somehow you did...

                    MEL
          And now you have so much love... so
          much wonderful love to give.

                    NELL
          Do I give you enough?

                    MEL
          So much and more. It's such a
          wonderful feeling... to really be
          loved. I mean, people always say "I
          love you" but what does it mean?
          There's so much more to it.

                    NELL
          Is that our love?

                                              (CONTINUED)

CONTINUED:

              MEL
It is.

              NELL
Come home and I will give you love.

              MEL
I want that love... so badly. I never want to leave that love again.

(Sirens again)

              MEL (CONT.)
What is that? What is going on? Is someone hurt?

              NELL
I don't hear them.

              MEL
They're getting closer.

              NELL
You'll be okay.

              MEL
I want to be with you.

(Sirens echo in the city... mix with ghostly cries)

              MEL (CONT.)
I'm so scared. I wish I knew where they were going.

              NELL
No where... they're going no where.

              MEL
That's how I feel... no where... going no where... without you it's no where.

              NELL
I felt that way before us. Sirens/cries fade.

              MEL
I love being a part of you.

              NELL
Like two halves...

(CONTINUED)

CONTINUED: 54.

> MEL
> ...that become one. You were made for me. I really believe you were made for me.

> NELL
> I am yours.

> MEL
> A gift from above... now that's worth flying for... to reach up high enough to catch you... A spirit in the clouds... my angel.

> NELL
> You're so sweet to me.

> MEL
> I hope so. You mean so much to me.

> NELL
> I better go now. Are you going to be okay?

> MEL
> I think so. It helps to see you... to hear you.

> NELL
> Is it enough?

> MEL
> I never get enough. The world is too demanding.

(The sirens again)

> NELL
> Don't let anything get in the way of us.

> MEL
> The world is screaming at me. I don't want to listen anymore.

(The sirens cry)

> NELL
> Then don't listen. Shut it out. Listen to my voice. Listen to my words... I love you.

(The sounds stop again)

(CONTINUED)

MEL
          Such sweet words. I love you.

                    NELL
          When you say them... yes.

                    MEL
          I miss you... so bad.

(Nell looks sad. Sirens start and lights flash red as they get closer. Mel looks at the lights and Nell tries to reach for him but can't. She cries and leaves)

                    MEL (CONT.)
          I always think I want to go
          somewhere but I am always sorry
          when I do. I thought I had to take
          a journey to find happiness, when
          in reality, happiness is at home
          with you. I guess the journeys make
          me appreciate you more. I journeyed
          so far, but the best thing was
          right at my door. Who would have
          thought that the best thing in the
          universe was only a walk away... no
          flying... no great voyage... just
          turn around and look... and ...
              (sees she is gone)
          That's something
          good, right? Just trying to find
          some good because I don't feel so
          good now.

(Sirens mix with cries)

                    MEL (CONT.) (cont'd)
          Alone. I hate being alone. The
          plane lifts me up but I feel like I
          am falling.
              (He falls to his knees)
          Falling away from you.

(He falls to the ground in a heap. There are sirens, red flashing lights, cries for help)

                    END OF SCENE

SCENE 14 - IF I LET MYSELF FALL

                NELL

If I let myself fall, will you catch me in your arms? Will you be there to soften my fall? Sometimes you have to fall to know if there is anyone there to catch you... to know if anyone cares.

I let myself fall because I trust you, I believe in you, I know you will always be there for me. You give me hope, bring me comfort, reach out to me in the darkness and show me the light. You are my guiding light that leads me from the darkness... saving me from the bottomless abyss of my soul.

Falling, falling... into never ending night. Endlessly lost in nothingness... Until you appear... Waiting for me... waiting to catch me in your arms and hold me so I never fall again.

             END OF SCENE

SCENE 15 - THE LAST CAN

(Mel and Nell are older and sitting in a basement that is a cross between a living room and a bomb shelter. There has been a nuclear war outside and they may be the last two people on Earth)

          NELL
What's wrong, luv?

          MEL
I'm hungry.

(Mel is staring at a can)

          NELL
Then eat. I don't mind.

          MEL
But it's the last one.

          NELL
It's okay.

          MEL
What about you? Aren't you hungry?

          NELL
Not really. He stares at it a long time.

          MEL
I can't believe it's the last one.

          NELL
It had to happen sooner or later.

          MEL
I was hoping for much later. He's looking for a can opener.

          NELL
Check under the table. Maybe it fell down there.

(While Mel is under the table, Nell rushes over and grabs the can and goes back to her chair, hiding the can. Mel gets up excited)

          MEL
Found it! Time to eat... sure you don't want...

(Mel stops when he sees the can is missing)

(CONTINUED)

CONTINUED: 58.

> MEL (CONT.)
> What is this! The hunger games!

(Mel sits on the sofa and looks at the empty coffee table)

> MEL (CONT.) (cont'd)
> Was I just imagining there was a can there? I am that hungry.

(Nell has a playful voice)

> NELL
> Maybe.

> MEL
> Or maybe someone took it.

(Mel leaps up suddenly and starts tickling Nell)

> NELL
> Stop, stop, you'll make me have to pee.

> MEL
> Hand it over!

> NELL
> Okay, okay.

(Nell holds up the can still laughing. Mel takes the can)

> MEL
> You sure you don't want any?

> NELL
> Nope.

(Mel opens the can and keeps his eyes on her. She is still giggling a bit. He has the can open but has no forks. He gets up to get a fork. Nell moves forward a bit)

> MEL
> Don't you dare. You'll make a mess.

(Nell laughs. Mel gets two forks and sits. Nell goes and sits by him. He feeds her a bite and she returns the favor)

> NELL
> The last can.

> MEL
> Afraid so.

(CONTINUED)

CONTINUED:

          NELL
Or maybe it is the first meal before the feast.

          MEL
The feast?

(They are still feeding each other)

          NELL
The feast that's waiting outside.

          MEL
Maybe the radiation fried up all the critters and turned them to jerky?

          NELL
Too bad you're a vegetarian.

          MEL
And all the fruit is all dried up and ready for consumption.

          NELL
And the water sparkles and bubbles like Perrier.

          MEL
But you don't like Perrier.

          NELL
I'll drink anything we can find that isn't plain old bottled water. I'm so sick of bottled water. I miss bubbles.

          MEL
I can make bubbles in your water.

          NELL
Ew, not those kind.

(They laugh. They feed each other more and then grow quiet)

          MEL
I wonder what it's really like outside.

          NELL
Not sure. The monitor still shows radiation.

(CONTINUED)

CONTINUED:

                MEL
We're out of food. Water is about out too.

                NELL
Time to start recycling.

                MEL
You don't mean... ew. I think I'd rather deal with the radiation.

(They are quiet a minute and finish the food)

                NELL
Thank you for sharing.

                MEL
Of course. I always do.

                NELL
You've always shared everything with me.

                MEL
You're my favorite person. I wanted to give you the best of everything... and the best of me.

                NELL
You always did... and you stayed with me to the end.

                MEL
It's not the end... not yet.

                NELL
I remember when they said the bombs were coming... I was all alone.

                MEL
I was terrified we wouldn't be together.

                NELL
Everyone was driving out of the city, trying to get far away from targets.

                MEL
I was driving the other way.

(CONTINUED)

CONTINUED:

> NELL
> They wanted to arrest you... force you to go.

> MEL
> Nothing was going to keep me from you.

> NELL
> I wasn't going in the shelter without you.

> MEL
> I remember I found you on the porch, sitting and looking up at the sky.

> NELL
> I wondered what it would have looked like... all the missiles in the sky.

> MEL
> I crashed the car in to that big tree in the yard.

> NELL
> I was so glad you weren't hurt. You scared me.

> MEL
> I was in a hurry. No time for brakes.

> NELL
> That would have been an ironic ending to your trip home. Crashing and dying.

> MEL
> I didn't have a scratch on me.

> NELL
> We were meant to be mole people together.

> MEL
> Burrowed together in our little nest.

> NELL
> I like our little nest.

(CONTINUED)

CONTINUED:

>   MEL
>   I think I've been happier here than
>   I've ever been before.
>
>   NELL
>   Me too.
>
>   MEL
>   No interruptions. No problems at
>   work. No outsiders getting their
>   noses in our business.
>
>   NELL
>   I never wanted to go outside again.
>
>   MEL
>   Except for the last can.
>
>   NELL
>   We made it over a year.
>
>   MEL
>   I could go longer.
>
>   NELL
>   Me too.
>
>   MEL
>   I wonder what the chair tastes
>   like.

(Mel goes to the chair)

>   NELL
>   That's my favorite chair! You're
>   not eating that.

(Mel removes the cushion)

>   NELL (CONT.)
>   What are you doing?
>
>   MEL
>   Seeing if you dropped any food down
>   here.
>
>   NELL
>   You should check your sofa. I'm a
>   much cleaner eater than you.
>
>   MEL
>   What?

(CONTINUED)

CONTINUED:

                    NELL
          You need a bib. That's why I feed
          you so you don't make a mess.

                    MEL
          Dang... you're right... no food
          here.

(Mel goes to the sofa and removes the cushion)

                    MEL (CONT.)
          Jackpot.

                    NELL
          Told you.

                    MEL
          Ha... veggie chips... I love these.

                    NELL
          Bon appetit.

                    MEL
          Merci.

(Mel munches on some veggie chips)

                    NELL
          How many are down there?

                    MEL
          A year's supply I think.

                    NELL
          You wish.

                    MEL
          If wishes were fishes...

                    NELL
          What does that mean?

                    MEL
          No clue.

(They laugh. Mel is munching on veggie chips. They grow quiet. Nell sits in her favorite chair)

                    NELL
          So what do we do?

(CONTINUED)

MEL
Go outside?

NELL
But the radiation.

MEL
We might have to risk it.

NELL
I wonder what it looks like outside.

MEL
Maybe all the bombs missed and it's all the same as before.

NELL
Then how do you explain the radiation?

MEL
You left the microwave on?

NELL
Maybe.

(They laugh. Nell is looking at a map now)

NELL (CONT.)
I wonder where we go?

MEL
Where was the last radio broadcast we heard?

NELL
That was awhile ago. I think I marked it on the map.

MEL
Some little station out in the boonies wasn't it?

NELL
Who would have thought that the last bits of civilization would be in some little town in the middle of nowhere?

MEL
Nowhere became the only somewhere.

(CONTINUED)

CONTINUED: 65.

>   NELL
>   I wonder how many people from the
>   city went there?
>
>   MEL
>   I bet there wasn't enough food to
>   go around.
>
>   NELL
>   Scary. What are the survivors going
>   to do for food?
>
>   MEL
>   Maybe we don't want to go out
>   there.
>
>   NELL
>   I know I don't want to.

(They are quiet)

>   MEL
>   I wonder how our shoes would taste?
>   Didn't Charlie Chaplin do that in a
>   movie?
>
>   NELL
>   I don't know any Chaplin. Heard of
>   him of course.
>
>   MEL
>   I'm amazed how many movies you do
>   know. It's kept me pretty
>   entertained.
>
>   NELL
>   Want me to perform another movie
>   for you?

(Mel laughs)

>   MEL
>   I think Jurassic Park is my
>   favorite. You do all the dinosaur
>   actions too.
>
>   NELL
>   I watched that one a lot as a kid.
>
>   MEL
>   I'm still amazed how well you
>   memorized them all.

(CONTINUED)

CONTINUED:

>   NELL
> One of my many special useless
> skills.
>
>   MEL
> Sure came in handy now.
>
>   NELL
> I guess it did, didn't it?
>
>   MEL
> You've kept me very entertained.
>
>   NELL
> I love what you wrote for me.
>
>   MEL
> I love what you drew for me.
>
>   NELL
> It's probably been the most
> creative time in my life.
>
>   MEL
> Me too. I wonder if anyone will
> ever see anything we did.
>
>   NELL
> It doesn't matter. I did it for
> you.
>
>   MEL
> You're very sweet to me. I can't
> imagine a better person to spend my
> life with.
>
>   NELL
> To be stuck with?
>
>   MEL
> I never felt stuck... even before
> we became mole people... you were
> the best choice I ever made.
>
>   NELL
> You're very sweet to me.
>
>   MEL
> You make me feel sweeter... I've
> never felt so happy.

(CONTINUED)

CONTINUED:

>   NELL
>   You've always taken good care of
>   me.
>
>   MEL
>   I never wanted to fail you.
>
>   NELL
>   You never did.
>
>   MEL
>   Until today...

(Nell goes to him)

>   NELL
>   What do you mean?
>
>   MEL
>   The food... it's gone.
>
>   NELL
>   But we probably had more food than
>   anyone else. You prepared so much
>   better than everyone else. You
>   always had everything covered...
>   you always took care of everything.
>
>   MEL
>   This is the first time I don't know
>   what to do. I never felt like this
>   before.
>
>   NELL
>   Like what?
>
>   MEL
>   Like I didn't know what to do...
>   how to solve the problem.
>
>   NELL
>   Maybe it's time you let someone
>   else handle everything.
>
>   MEL
>   You have a plan?
>
>   NELL
>   No, but I bet someone else does.

(Nell points up)

(CONTINUED)

CONTINUED:

>   MEL
>   Oh... I've always admired your
>   faith.
>
>   NELL
>   We've done well so far.
>
>   MEL
>   We have.
>
>   NELL
>   I have a feeling something is going
>   to happen. Something good.
>
>   MEL
>   You know... I believe you. I really
>   believe you.
>
>   NELL
>   I don't know what or how... but
>   something good will happen.
>
>   MEL
>   I believe.
>
>   NELL
>   Then close your eyes and get on
>   your knees.
>
>   MEL
>   We're going to pray?
>
>   NELL
>   Yes, pray.

(Mel gets down on his knees at the coffee table. He closes his eyes and prays silently. Nell sneaks off)

>   MEL
>   I know I don't pray as often as a I
>   should, but I really want to now,
>   more than ever... rather than
>   begging for something... I want to
>   thank you for giving us this
>   wonderful year together... I'm so
>   thankful we got to be with each
>   other... you've given me this
>   wonderful gift and she is the most
>   precious gift I've even been
>   given... I thank you for her... I
>   thank you with all my heart.

(CONTINUED)

CONTINUED: 69.

(Nell has come back during this and smiles so happily at his words. She places a box of donut cake type things in front of him)

                MEL (CONT.)
Amen.

(He opens his eyes and sees her smiling happily and she points to the box. Mel laughs)

              MEL (CONT.) (cont'd)
You're an angel.

(Mel hugs her happily)

                  NELL
I saved the best for last.

(Suddenly music is heard)

                  MEL
Do you hear that?

                  NELL
That's the intercom.

                  MEL
It's picking up music from outside. Someone's playing music.

                  NELL
Beautiful, beautiful music.

                  MEL
Should we go see?

                  NELL
Maybe they're after our Diddly Doos?

                  MEL
Nothing is getting my Diddly Doos.

(Nell gets a pouty face)

              MEL (CONT.)
Except you of course.

(She smiles happily. The music gets louder)

                  NELL
It's coming closer.

                                (CONTINUED)

MEL
I feel like a kid hearing an ice cream truck.

NELL
Maybe it is an ice cream truck.

MEL
I like Diddly Doos better.

NELL
Yummy... ice cream.

MEL
Should we go see?

NELL
Okay.

MEL
Ready?

NELL
Let me get my sweater.

(She gets her sweater)

MEL
Ah... that's such a cute sweater.

NELL
Thank you.

MEL
Ready?

NELL
I'm a little scared.

MEL
I'll be with you.

NELL
Promise.

MEL
I promise. I'll never leave you.

NELL
You never do.

(CONTINUED)

CONTINUED:

                        MEL
          Let's go.

(They go off stage and sounds of a massive door unlocking and opening. Music gets much louder. After a moment, Mel rushes back in and gets the box of donut/cake things and then runs off again)

                    END OF PLAY

CAST OF CHARACTERS

MEL - a kind man who was unhappy until he met the perfect woman although internal fears hold him back at times

NELL - a quirky woman who is in love with Mel because of his kindness and how happy he makes her (most of the time)

JAY* - friend of Mel

LISSY* - woman on the subway who reads trashy romance novels but wishes she'd find love

MARIO* - a restaurant waiter dressed like the video game character

BATMAN* - waiter dressed as the superhero

MIME* - silent waiter dressed as a traditional mime

CLOWN* - waiter who is British, sad and dressed as a clown

CARL* - Mel's car mechanic and unofficial psychologist

HIPSTERS* - around 4 hipster hobos who hang out in a cafe looking cool (number of hipsters can vary - the more the better)

*Actors may play multiple roles with the exception of Mel and Nell

****

For permission to perform this play, contact doug@freedrama.net (please include the title "When Mel Fell for Nell" in the request).

Copyright (c) 2015

All Rights Reserved

Cover art by Shiela Larson

**** (cont'd)

BONUS MONOLOGUES BY SHIELA LARSON

"Mama" by Shiela Larson

NELL

Oh child,

Why do you insist on waking me up at night?

Why do you act like a cat and poop in something I've just cleaned for you?

Or make messes in the kitchen and play with the pots and pans thinking you're in a band?

Why do you poke my face with your finger covered in banana?

Why do I put up with it?

Because when you look at me with those big eyes, and say "Mama", it makes it all worth it.

****

"Fear and Love" by Shiela Larson

NELL

When I first saw you it wasn't love at first sight, it was more like "Hey how's it going?". We became friends and had our own lives, never did I think we had so much in common. One day I began to notice you more and more, I started to see how you really were. You wanted people to think you were one thing but I saw through it. You were very kind, misunderstood, and were in need of love. It occurred to me you were in danger, holding on by a thread and needed to be sewed back together. Going against what my brain was thinking and going with my heart and soul I decided to pursue you. People judged, gossiped, and outright hated us. Trying to pull us apart, they were almost successful. The fear in us,

(MORE)

(CONTINUED)

                    NELL (cont'd)
          the "What if's?" and "Why are we
          doing this?" swarmed our minds. No
          matter where we went it followed.
          Finally we broke, pieces of us were
          scattered around us. Trying to put
          myself back together I felt it was
          unsuccessful, I needed one last
          part to my life, you. Starting to
          think about being with you made me
          scared, the biggest thought was the
          idea of breaking apart again. Love
          is a scary part of life, the best
          and the worst is brought out of
          love. I felt that I would rather be
          scared than broken for the rest of
          my life. Now I feel whole, being
          held together by glue, most likely
          there will be cracks in this love,
          but the glue will put it back
          together again. Fear will never go
          away, it will always rear it's ugly
          face around. The fear is different
          now. I've come to accept it but at
          the same time dread the idea. The
          idea that I know one day you will
          be gone. This fear makes me feel
          weak, to know there is nothing I
          can do to stop it. The only thing I
          can do is make the most of what we
          have now and prepare myself for the
          future.

                    END OF MONOLOGUE

                         ***

Printed in Great Britain
by Amazon.co.uk, Ltd.,
Marston Gate.